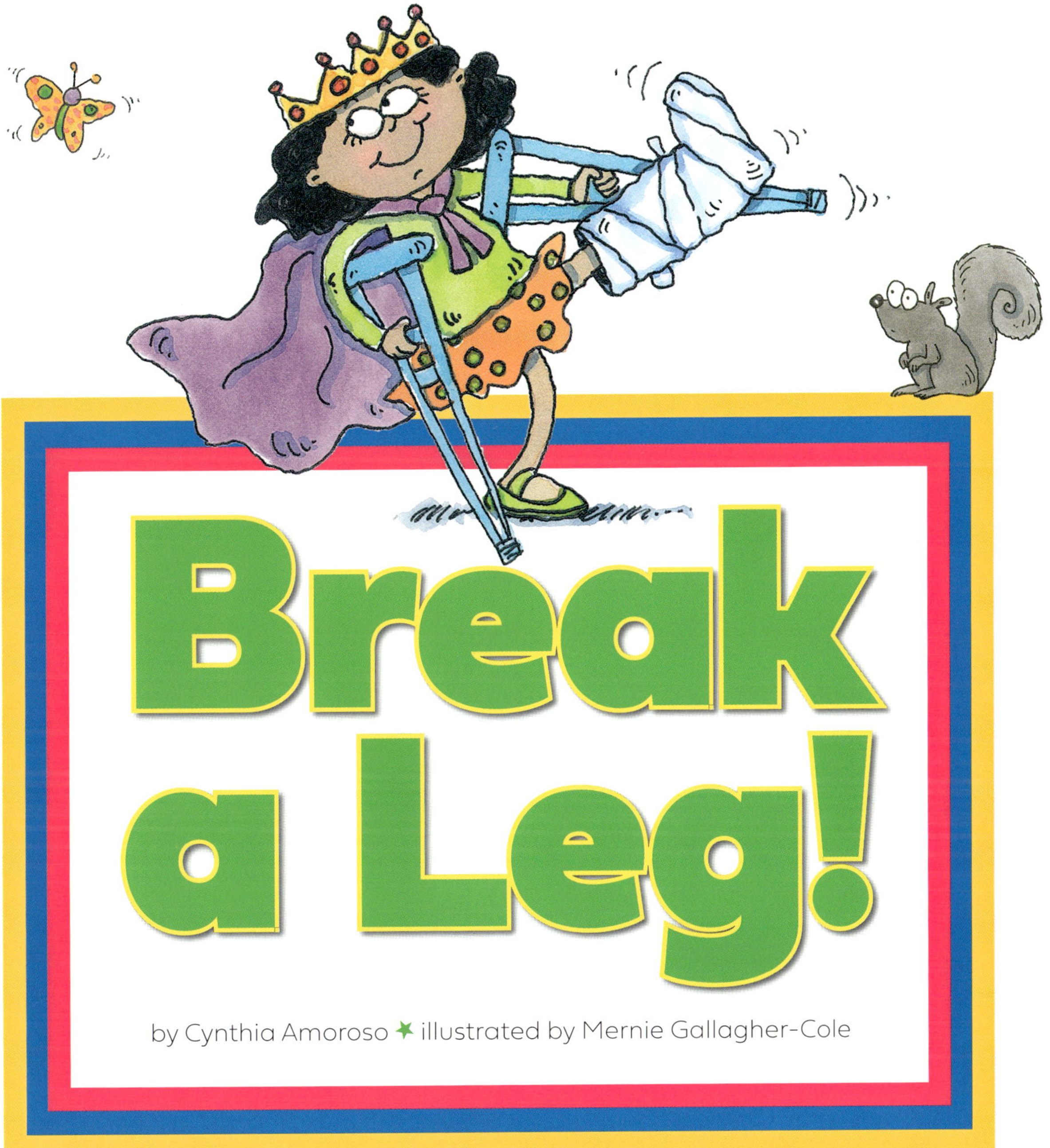

Break a Leg!

by Cynthia Amoroso ✶ illustrated by Mernie Gallagher-Cole

Wonder Books

An Imprint of The Child's World®

childsworld.com

Published by The Child's World®
800-599-READ • childsworld.com

ISBN Information
9781503865594 (Reinforced Library Binding)
9781503866041 (Portable Document Format)
9781503866881 (Online Multi-user eBook)
9781503867727 (Electronic Publication)

LCCN 2022939527

Printed in the United States of America

ABOUT THE AUTHOR

As a daughter of elementary and English teachers, Cynthia Amoroso grew up in a home that was filled with language. She spent many hours enjoying reading and writing. Later, she followed in the footsteps of both her parents and became a teacher. As a high school English teacher and as an elementary teacher, Cynthia shared her love of language with students. She has always been fascinated with idioms and other figures of speech as they reflect and represent the culture and people who use them.

ABOUT THE ILLUSTRATOR

Mernie Gallagher-Cole lives in Pennsylvania with her husband and children. She uses idioms like the ones in this book every day. She has illustrated many children's books as well as greeting cards, puzzles, and games.

Contents

People use **idioms** every day. These are sayings and phrases with meanings that are different from the actual words. Some idioms seem silly. Many of them don't make much sense . . . at first.

This book will help you understand some of the most common idioms. The illustrations will show you how you might hear a saying or phrase. And the accompanying examples and definitions will tell you how the idiom is used, what it really means, and where it **originated**. All of these idioms—even the silly or humorous ones—are a rich, colorful part of the English language. You'll soon see that understanding idioms and knowing how to use them is a piece of cake!

Break a leg

Cora had the lead in the school play. She knew all her lines, but she was still nervous. The first performance was about to start. She took a deep breath to calm herself. The director walked by to check Cora's costume for the last time. Then he gave Cora a big grin and said, "You're all set. Break a leg!"

MEANING: *Good luck; a way of wishing a performer well*

ORIGIN: *This* ***expression*** *comes from the* ***superstition*** *that wishing a performer good luck before a show will actually bring them bad luck—so you wish them bad luck instead!*

Chew the fat

It was lunchtime, and Stuart was hungry. His mom had stepped outside a little while ago. Finally she came back in.

"Hi, Mom," said Stuart. "Could we make lunch? I'm starved!"

"Sure!" said his mom with a smile. "Sorry I took so long. I was chewing the fat with the neighbors. They just got back from vacation, and I wanted to hear how it went."

MEANING: *To talk or chat with someone*

ORIGIN: *Many believe this saying originated in the military in the late 1800s. Service members were given meals of tough meat. They had to chew through the fat of their meat as they talked to each other while they ate.*

Come to a head

Rob wasn't in a good mood. He'd just come home from baseball practice.

"What's the matter?" his sister asked.

"Oh," said Rob, "Zach and Michael got really mad and yelled at each other. They haven't been getting along very well lately. Today, everything came to a head."

MEANING: *When a situation has been developing and finally reaches a crisis point*

ORIGIN: *This phrase gained popularity in the 1600s. The "head" most often referred to a painful sore on the body (such as an ulcer or boil) that was about to burst open. Farmers also used this phrase as they waited for cabbage leaves to grow together and form a head.*

Down-to-the-wire

Chris and Rachel were helping their friend Sam run for class president. She was running against a classmate named Matthew. Both of the candidates were very popular.

"What a close race!" said Chris, as he put up a "Vote for Sam!" poster. "Do you think Sam is going to win?"

"I don't know," said Rachel. "I think it's going to come down-to-the-wire."

MEANING: *At the last minute; running out of time*

ORIGIN: *This saying became popular in the 1940s. The "wire" refers to the finish line in horse racing, which marks the end of the race.*

Easy as pie

Jordan and Sue went canoeing for the first time with their uncle Mark. He showed them how to paddle and steer, and they paddled all over the lake.

"How was it?" asked Aunt Tess as the three came in for lunch.

"Great!" said Sue. "It's so much fun!"

"It isn't hard, either," said Jordan. "In fact, it's easy as pie!"

MEANING: *Very easy; not difficult*

ORIGIN: *Many believe the phrase became popular in the United States in the 1800s. The author Mark Twain often used the word* pie *to refer to something that was pleasant. Other American writings around that time used the phrase "like eating pie," which meant something that was easy to accomplish.*

Fly-by-night

Tim's neighbor had just hired a company to put a new front door on his house. When Tim came outside, his neighbor was looking at the door with a frown on his face.

"What's wrong?" Tim asked.

"They didn't do a very good job installing my door," said his neighbor. "And now I can't get them to fix it. What a fly-by-night company!"

MEANING: *Someone who doesn't do things well and might not stay in business for long; an* ***unreliable*** *person*

ORIGIN: *In ancient times, this term referred to a woman who was thought to be a witch (many believed that witches flew through the skies at night). In the 1800s, the phrase was used to describe a person who snuck away during the night to avoid finishing a job or paying a debt.*

Get into the swing of things

Josh had been sick, and it was his first day back at school. He couldn't believe how much schoolwork he had missed.

"Don't be discouraged," said his dad at dinner that night. "You've been gone all week. It'll take you a few days to get back in the swing of things."

MEANING: *To feel comfortable doing something*

ORIGIN: *The phrase "in full swing" first appeared in the 1500s. It simply meant to be active in something. Eventually the phrase grew into "get into the swing of things" and became popular in the 1800s.*

Graveyard shift

Jenna ran into the house. "I'm home!" she hollered as she slammed the door.

Her dad looked up from reading his book. "Shh! Your mom's still sleeping, Jenna."

"Why is she sleeping?" asked Jenna. "It's almost lunchtime!"

"One of the people she works with got sick last night," explained Dad. "So your mom went in and worked the graveyard shift."

MEANING: *A block of time that somebody works at night, usually from midnight to dawn*

ORIGIN: *This term first appeared in the late 1800s. In those days, the owners of factories realized that they could increase production if they kept operations running 24 hours a day. (This was before there were laws protecting workers.) The idea of a graveyard* ***symbolizes*** *being alone and a quiet place. The term came to mean being out and about when most other people were asleep.*

Hit the hay

Erica was curled up on the sofa. She wanted to watch the end of the movie, but she was getting really sleepy.

"You look like you're ready for bed," said her mom.

"I think I can make it to the end," Erica replied sleepily.

"Mom's right. It's late. Let's watch the rest tomorrow," said Dad. "It's time to hit the hay."

MEANING: *To go to bed*

ORIGIN: *This* ***slang*** *expression became popular in the United States in the 1930s. People (mostly men) who traveled the country and worked odd jobs would often find themselves spending the night outside or in someone's barn. They would use hay to make a soft bed. After working outside all day, a worker was exhausted and would fall asleep as soon as their head "hit the hay."*

In a nutshell

Kyle's family was hoping to move from their small apartment into a house. They'd found one they really liked, with a park nearby and a great yard. Kyle's parents were meeting with the owner. When they came home, Kyle and his sisters were waiting.

"How did it go? Did we get it?" they asked excitedly.

"In a nutshell," said Dad, "pack your bags!"

MEANING: *To give a short answer or just the basic information; clear and to the point*

ORIGIN: *The phrase was first used by an ancient Roman philosopher. He described seeing a copy of a poem written in such tiny print that the* ***parchment*** *could fit inside a nutshell. Over time, the phrase eventually came to mean "briefly" or "to the point."*

Out of the frying pan and into the fire

Jason was writing an adventure story. The hero had just escaped from evil aliens, and Jason wasn't sure what should come next.

"Well," said his mom, "how about putting him in even greater danger?"

"Hmm," said Jason, thinking hard. "So he escapes from the aliens and thinks he's safe, but then—look out! Things get even worse!"

"Yup," said Mom. "Out of the frying pan and into the fire."

MEANING: *To get out of a bad situation only to end up in an even worse one*

ORIGIN: *Something in a frying pan is very hot, but something in a fire is even hotter! This expression has been popular since ancient times. Most agree its first printed use was in an English pamphlet in the 1500s.*

Pass the buck

Everybody was getting ready for the school party. Ms. Flynn's class was putting up decorations.

"Hey, Joe," said Nathaniel, from his perch on a stepstool. "Could you go to Mr. Dillon's classroom and get the streamers?"

"Can't," answered Joe. "I'm busy. Ask Emma."

"I'm busy, too," Emma said. "Try Kaitlin."

"Come on, you guys," Nathaniel said with a sigh. "Please, somebody grab the streamers. Quit passing the buck!"

MEANING: *To hand a* **responsibility** *on to someone else; to have someone else make a decision*

ORIGIN: *In the 1800s, a "buck" was something passed to the dealer in a poker game. Eventually the phrase came to mean shifting responsibility to another person.*

Play it by ear

Tomorrow was the Fourth of July, and Angela's family was trying to decide what to do.

"We could go to the fireworks," suggested Hannah.

"We could go to the lake," said Maria.

"There's a big parade in town," suggested Mom. "That's always fun."

"The weather forecast says it might rain," said Dad. "Why don't we see what it's like tomorrow morning? Let's play it by ear."

MEANING: *To wait and see what happens; to make plans as you go*

ORIGIN: *This saying became popular in the 1600s, and it originally referred to music. It meant you could play a song on an instrument by recalling its melody, not by looking at the sheet music. Over time the phrase also came to mean to "**improvise** without planning ahead."*

Pull your leg

Amy and her little brother, Brandon, were spending time with their grandpa. Brandon was showing Grandpa what a silly face he could make.

"Careful, Brandon," said Grandpa. "If you do that too often, your face will stay that way!"

"Really?" said Brandon, his eyes wide.

"Oh Grandpa, you used to tell me that, too," Amy said with a laugh. "Don't worry, Brandon. Grandpa's just pulling your leg."

MEANING: *To tease people by telling them something that isn't true*

ORIGIN: *In the late 1800s people would sometimes trip others for fun by catching their legs with a cane or running string across a walkway. It was meant to be a joke. At times, robbers would use this tactic to steal from people. Eventually the phrase came to mean "**deceiving** someone in a fun or playful way."*

The real McCoy

Ben had just gotten home from a baseball game at the stadium. He was very excited!

"Hey Carl," he said to his brother. "Take a look at this!" He held up a baseball.

"Did you catch a ball?" cried Carl.

"I sure did. I got it signed, too!" Ben exclaimed.

"Wow, really?" said Carl.

"It's the real McCoy," said Ben, smiling.

MEANING: *The real thing, genuine; not a fake or a copy*

ORIGIN: *There is debate on the true origin of this idiom. Some experts claim this refers to an inventor named Elijah McCoy. In the early 1900s, he invented a part for the steam engine. It was so successful that others tried to copy his work. So he would make sure his customers would look for the "real McCoy."*

Sick as a dog

"Will, where are you? We're going to be late," yelled Travis. He tapped his foot as he waited impatiently by the front door. He looked up to see his mom walking down the stairs.

"Where's Will? We're going to be late for school if we don't leave now!" said Travis.

"Will is staying home today. He's sick as a dog!" answered Mom.

MEANING: *Very sick*

ORIGIN: *This popular* ***simile*** *dates back to the 1500s. The exact origin is uncertain, but some say that the phrase started because diseases were often spread to humans by animals such as rats, birds, and dogs.*

Spitting image

Joy's grandma lived far away, and Joy didn't get to see her very often. Finally, Grandma was coming for a visit. Joy was so excited! Joy ran to her grandma the second she saw her walking up their driveway.

"Why, Joy!" said Grandma with a laugh. "You're the spitting image of your Aunt Kristin!"

MEANING: *Someone who looks very much like someone else; an exact likeness*
ORIGIN: *The original saying was "spit and image," because the word* spit *was a shorter version of* spirit, *which meant "likeness." Over time the phrase became popular and was shortened to "spitting image."*

Sweet tooth

Ruben and his sister were at a picnic. There was a table full of tasty food—hamburgers, hot dogs, chips, potato salad, and lots more. They finished off one plateful and went back for more.

"Look what Maddy's up to," said Ruben. "All she's been eating are brownies, cookies, and cake."

"I know," said Ruben's sister. "That kid really has a sweet tooth!"

MEANING: *A liking for sweet foods*
ORIGIN: *This term can be traced back to the 1300s. Most people believe that "sweet tooth" comes from the word* toothsome, *which means "delicious" or "tasty."*

Throw in the towel

Olivia's soccer team had lost their last three games. The other teams had outscored them easily. Olivia wasn't looking forward to playing today. "Maybe we should just quit," she said to her teammate.

The team gathered around their coach before the game. "All right," the coach said. "I know we've lost some games, and I'm sure you feel like throwing in the towel. But I believe you can win this one!"

MEANING: *To quit or give up*

ORIGIN: *This popular phrase came from the sport of boxing in Great Britain during the 1800s. If a boxer was getting badly beaten in a fight, the manager or coach would toss a towel or sponge into the ring to stop the match. The fight would then be over. "Throwing in the towel" soon came to mean that you were admitting defeat.*

Two cents

Dana, Kristal, and Gina couldn't decide what to do. "My mom said she'd take us to a movie," said Dana.

"It's nice today," said Kristal. "I'd rather go to the park and play."

"We do that all the time," said Dana.

"Excuse me," said Gina. "Could I put in my two cents? I think we should do both."

MEANING: *Your opinion; what you think about something*

ORIGIN: *The term "two cents" came from poker games during the 1800s. In order to play the card game, a person had to put in their two-cent (or "two-bit") bet. Eventually the phrase "putting in your two cents" came to mean stating your opinion about something.*

When in Rome

"This is weird," whispered Tim. "Where's the butter? Where's the syrup?" He stared at his waffle. He and his family were on vacation, eating breakfast in a restaurant far from home.

"See the toppings in those dishes?" asked his dad. "You put those on your waffle."

"That's weird," Tim replied. "Why don't they make them like we do at home?"

"Come on, give it a try," said Dad. "When in Rome . . ."

MEANING: *Do what is typical or customary in a certain place or setting, especially if you are a visitor*

ORIGIN: *The full* **proverb** *is this: "When in Rome, do as the Romans do." This means that when you're in another place, you should try things the way people do them there. Adapt to the customs or traditions of a new place. The expression can be traced back to letters from 300 AD.*

Glossary

deceiving (dih-SEE-ving): To make someone believe something that isn't true; giving a false impression.

expression (ek-SPREH-shun): A common saying; telling or showing your thoughts and feelings.

idioms (ID-ee-umz): Phrases or sayings whose meaning can't be understood by their individual words taken separately.

improvise (IM-pruh-vize): To make, recite, or invent on the spot without planning or preparing beforehand.

originated (uh-RIJ-ih-nay-ted): To bring or come into being; to begin.

parchment (PARCH-munt): Paper-like material made from animal skins, such as sheep or goats.

proverb (PRAH-vurb): A popular, often short saying that expresses something true and wise.

responsibility (ree-spon-suh-BIL-uh-tee): Being reliable and accountable for something; carrying the burden for something.

simile (SIM-uh-lee): A figure of speech comparing two things using like or as. For example, "shine like a star" is a simile.

slang (SLANG): Informal speech; giving new meanings to old words or inventing new words.

superstition (soo-pur-STIH-shun): A belief or practice that isn't grounded in facts; trust in magic or chance.

symbolizes (SIM-buh-lye-zez): To serve as a symbol of; to stand for something.

unreliable (un-ruh-LYE-uh-bul): Not dependable or reliable; not trustworthy.

Wonder More

- Write a short story using an idiom. You can make up a story or use an experience from your own life. For example, if you choose the idiom "every cloud has a silver lining," you could write about discovering something good in an otherwise bad situation.

- In what ways do idioms impact our writing? In your opinion, do they help improve our ability to tell stories and describe events, or are they unnecessary? Explain your reasoning.

- Think of an idiom that isn't in this book and create a new entry. Write your own brief story using the idiom, and draw a picture to go with it. Then write down its meaning and origin. If you don't know the idiom's origin, where could you learn more about it?

- The idiom "when in Rome" from this book is about being adaptable and open-minded. Partner with someone in your class and talk about this popular saying. Use the idiom to start a discussion on the importance of embracing differences and welcoming new ideas and opinions. Can you think of examples from your own life when you did this?

Find Out More

In the Library

Fiedler, Heidi, and Kearney, Brendan (illustrator). *The Know-Nonsense Guide to Grammar: An Awesomely Fun Guide to the Way We Use Words!* Laguna Beach, CA: Walter Foster, 2022.

Heinrichs, Ann. *Similes and Metaphors.* Mankato, MN: The Child's World, 2020.

Pearson, Yvonne, and Mernie Gallagher-Cole (illustrator). *Rev Up Your Writing in Fictional Stories.* Mankato, MN: The Child's World, 2016.

Schubert, Susan, and Raquel Bonita (illustrator). *I'll Believe You When . . . Unbelievable Idioms from around the World.* Minneapolis, MN: Lerner, 2020.

On the Web

Visit our website for links about idioms: **childsworld.com/links**

Note to Parents, Caregivers, Teachers, and Librarians: We routinely verify our Web links to make sure they are safe and active sites. So encourage your readers to check them out!

Index